Donal

GW01090681

Pilgrim 2000

Advent & Christmas 1999

the columba press

First published in 1999 by
the columba press
55A Spruce Avenue, Stillorgan Industrial Park,
Blackrock, Co Dublin

Cover by Bill Bolger
Origination by The Columba Press
Printed in Ireland by Colour Books Ltd, Dublin

ISBN 1 85607 280 0

Preface

Any spirituality of the millennium and Jubilee of the Lord's incarnation is based on hope. A Jubilee looks back on the main events of what it celebrates and takes from it what brings hope for the future. *Pilgrim 2000* celebrates the Jubilee of the Lord Jesus' birth with prayer and reflections on Jubilee themes centred on hope. In a spirituality of the Jubilee of the birth of Christ, themes of witness, celebration, reconciliation, justice and joy are essential elements of this hope.

Pilgrim 2000 is a celebration of the witness over the centuries of committed people whose lives were connected intimately to the following of Christ. These are people known as saints or remembered in our own family or friendship circles, or in the circles of religious community or parish. Their memory is like an injection of hope today. We rejoice in their witness and hope that, by touching into the reality of witness in people's lives, our own witness will be enhanced and our commitment deepened. Jubilee spirituality both celebrates witness and calls us to witness to Jesus in our lives.

A time of Jubilee involves looking back as well as looking forward. We hope that our reconciliation with others and ourselves will be deepened. It's a time to let go into the hands of God what needs forgiveness and healing. We ask for forgiveness and reconciliation for the evil and the sin which has been done in the name of God and of the church. Jubilee is a time for personal forgiveness, and is a celebration of and a call to reconciliation. Real hope among us is based on a willingness to let go of what makes for bitterness and selfishness.

Similarly with justice. A Jubilee calls us to give every one his or her rights. It has often been a time of cancelling debts, particularly debts incurred unjustly. In celebration of the life of Jesus and discipleship of 2000 years, we sense a call to work with him for a more just world. Our call to justice is to build in the world a lasting peace based on justice, so that more of the people of the world may live in hope.

Joy and thanks are strands of all Jubilee celebrations. We thank God for the life of Jesus and all that has been done in his name. We thank God for all he has done for each of us in Jesus' name. Our Jubilee liturgies will celebrate this joy and thanks in music, word, activity and the attitude of our hearts. Our hope as Christians is a hope that grounds confidence in life, and is based on the promise of Jesus that love from God never ceases, that in God we are brothers and sisters, and that peace and justice and goodness will overcome the evil of the world.

November 28 SETTING THE STAGE OF PREPARATION
2000 years ago, Jesus Christ was born among us. The Son of God became one like us, the Word of God was made flesh – born in time, born in history, born of Mary. For 2000 years this man has influenced the lives of millions of people, baptised to be his disciples. For 2000 years, through his church and followers, he has influenced more than anyone else the course of history. People have lived by his name and died for his name, in the faith that they will rise in his name. We prepare to celebrate this birth and bring our gifts to the child of Bethlehem: gifts of reconciliation, gifts of love, lives founded on justice and peace, faith and compassion, confidence and hope.
Lord, may we and all your church
draw closer to you in the year of Jubilee,
and serve you more faithfully.

November 29 JOY OF GIVING
There is a great joy in knowing that we have helped someone in life. We meet someone we taught in school and we're told that something we said or did really stood to them in later life. Or we listened at a bad time to someone in real trouble and a burden was lifted and life seemed brighter. How many parents have made endless sacrifices for children and feel the joy that comes from their generosity at a time like graduation or marriage? There is a joy in giving that only givers know. We all desire that joy – the human need to love is not just to receive love, but to give love. Some of the loneliest people are those who have nobody to love. This joy of giving may be painful and may drain us of what we need ourselves. Jesus knew that when he said the words that have echoed for two thousand years: 'I have come that you may have joy and have it to the full.'
Lord may I look for joy
in places that are true
and in love and service.

November 30 RECONCILED WITH SELF

Reconciliation means being able to forgive ourselves and move on in freedom, without being a prisoner of guilt. Sometimes we move out of destructive or sinful behaviour but feel guilty forever. There's a bit of ourselves that we cannot accept or befriend. People who hit drugs, who gamble, who are ashamed of some aspect of their past, may be trapped forever in what once happened. Reconciliation with ourselves means full acceptance of what we did – even the harm we did – and then trying to make up for what happened if we can, and living in greater freedom. It means being able to see ourselves whole as children of God, loved and forgiven and called now into service with God. It's like a trap opened and what's imprisoned is set free. The free spirit is free in the influence of the Spirit of God reconciling us to all the bits and pieces of ourselves.

Lord, may I look on myself as you do,
seeing all my past and all my present,
and giving myself to your plan for my future.

December 1 A KINDNESS REMEMBERED

At the age of eight I got on the wrong train. Wanting to go from one station to another in Dublin, I ended up on the Athlone train and panicked. I was in tears – just lost and not knowing what to do. I remember well the panic – and the kindness. Simple acts of kindness from simple people. A Franciscan Brother on the train produced comfort – kind words, a handkerchief to dry my tears, an apple and some sweets. The station-master rang my father from Athlone and told him where I was, and then brought me to his home and gave me my tea. I was put on the mail train home. Witness is a big word for kindness to a lost child. With such actions is the gospel kept alive. Jesus lives in 2000 AD and a lost child was found with love.

Lord bless all who help others
In small ways of kindness;
may I do the same myself.

December 2 'WINCING' WITH CHRIST

Some of the poverty and hardship we see has little answer. Tens of thousands of refugees – victims of a war they know little about – or children born into poverty never chosen. And we think that with a more sensible distribution of the world's resources, such hardship need not be. A country, which can barely provide food, spends money on nuclear weapons. If we think about it long enough, we get angry, lash out our rage and feel helpless, feel guilty; we wince in sympathy at the pain of others. The only answer from God may be something like, 'I wince too, as I winced when they tortured my Son.' We need to allow ourselves time to wince in prayer at the injustice which makes life a sort of hell for so many people.

Lord, you are cut to the heart
at the sufferings of so many.
Make my heart like yours.

December 3 CELEBRATION

There's a lot to celebrate in our Christianity. We think of all that has been done in the name of Jesus – the schools and hospitals founded, and millions cared for, the places of encouragement and of prayer that kept people going in life. We have a lot to be grateful for. And we celebrate not just what has been done in the name of Jesus but we celebrate Jesus himself. Like we say at a party for someone – we just want to celebrate *you.* We celebrate the One who came from God to walk our ways on earth. One who laughed like us and suffered like us. One who was fully part of our lives and related to people in ways that made everyone feel he or she mattered. Let's think of Jesus and smile, just as the memory of a friend brings a lift to our steps or a light to our eyes. Celebrating Jesus means being grateful for who he is in himself. But Jesus won't leave it at that. When we celebrate him, he would say, 'When you celebrate me, you celebrate every man and woman who lives.'

Lord Jesus, make us truly grateful
for who you are, Son of God and Mary,
and then grateful that each of us is a child of God.

December 4 AWAITING JUBILEE

About twelve months before the Jubilee, people said that
every hotel was booked out for 31 December. And almost all
the taxis were already booked, and buses. There is preparation
to celebrate New Year's Eve 1999. Like for any jubilee celebration, we prepare for the event. For a family jubilee, people
might gather all the family photos into an album to present to
a jubilee couple. A jubilee doesn't just happen. Time and love
goes into making it happen and making it memorable. There
is something to look forward to. In the Jubilee 2000 can we
look forward to getting to know Jesus better, serving him especially in the poor and the really needy in our world, and enjoying what he came on earth to do: 'to bring life and bring it
to the full'? Can we look forward to debt being lightened for
poor nations?

Lord, help me to know you more,
love you more
and serve you more faithfully in my life.

December 5 THE JOY OF THANKS

Gratitude is like the fragrance of scented oil in a bath of water.
It flows through all the water, noticed only by its scent. And
even in a bath of dirty water, it will give its fragrance. No matter what the circumstances of life, the grace of God through
Jesus Christ, is offered as a strength and a fragrance of life. In
good times, tough times, tragedies and losses, the life of God
is always near. A grateful attitude is a sure foundation for the
Christian life, for it was the foundation of the life of Christ. It
is a sure foundation of joy and of hope. 'Thanks' is a word
spoken and sung, danced and ritualised in many ways, con-
tinuously, in our jubilees.

Lord make me truly grateful
for who I am, just now,
and who you are, just now.

December 6 HIS HOME IN US

We need a place called home, a place of acceptance, celebration, of love, of feeling safe. A place to be loved. And to love. A place to move out from. Where we learn lessons of the heart, and truths not just to adhere to but to live by. Home may be our family group or another network, in which we live and move and have our being. And God was something the same. Was heaven too far away for him? When Jesus talks of home, he talks of making his home within you and me. We look for God in many places – creation, sacraments, understanding, but the deepest home of God is in you and me. There he finds a place in the world, a place to be accepted and he wants that. And it is from there that he moves out. Without a place in you and me, God is remote and uninvolved with people. The only way he works today within the world is through you and me, and all his people, in whom he has found a home. We are witnesses that God is at home in the world.

Lord Jesus, make your home in me;
reveal the depths of love in me where you live
and together may we share this love today.

December 7 JUBILEE THANKS

At any jubilee celebration, we thank the jubilarians. In a family, a religious community, a business group – any group where we meet for a jubilee. And the same with the Jubilee of Jesus' birth. We thank God for what he has done in Jesus. And we know that we are thanking for a continuous event, for God 'sees and loves in us what he sees and loves in Jesus'. The Jubilee will be an empty year if we are grateful only to the Jesus of 2000 years ago. We are thanking for the Jesus of the year 2000, and for 2000 years of life, death and resurrection within his church and within all the people of God. For what we do in his name, he does in us; what he does in our name, we do in him.

Lord, thank you for your birth,
for your life, death and resurrection,
now and always.

December 8 RAISES THE LOWLY

Much energy has gone into the cancellation of debts of poorer to richer nations. Education and health care has been effected by the huge debts owed to the rich nations, and when education and health are effected, it is the poor who suffer. The concentration of the energies of many people on the cancellation of debt is an activity of the Holy Spirit, and an energy of the Spirit. Anyone who is involved in trying to better the conditions of the poor by the cancellation of debts is engaged in the work and love of Jesus. These are the people Mary sings of in her prayer of praise: 'he casts the mighty from the thrones and raises the lowly.'

Lord Jesus, break the chains of debt;
break the chains of hunger, poverty and misery;
be with those who try to break these chains.

December 9 FORGIVEN AND RECONCILED?

It's probably true to say that it's easier to forgive than to be reconciled. Forgiveness is of course a big grace and very unselfish. And it's no mean feat! In the love of God there is something more – God remakes the relationship and we move into deeper love and friendship. When we forgive we often feel we don't want to be hurt again. So we say, 'I'll not hold this against you, but I don't really want to meet you again.' And sometimes this is as much as we can do. Reconciliation makes its own demands – for apology, repentance, sorrow, some form of restitution, and a wish on both sides of a quarrel to make things up and to make things better. This whether it's between individuals or between communities which have been divided. Reconciliation opens the door to deep joy and freedom, for every bitterness or unreconciled bit of our being is a like a trap which trips us up on our Christian journey.

Lord Jesus, in you we see forgiveness
and we know the grace of reconciliation.
Open wide the space of reconciliation in our hearts.

December 10 JOY OF COURAGE

There's joy in courageously facing up to difficulties in life. We can look back over a time when family life was rough – when a child was ill or in trouble, when finances were not so healthy, and we see we got through. And the relationship of the couple grew stronger. Or family life blossomed. The same maybe after death and other losses. It's a different type of joy from the laughter of a sing-song or a very happy joy. It is no less real. It's a joy with a deep smile rather than a belly-laugh. It's like the joy of Jesus after the resurrection – he knew he had been through pain, and death and sorrow. He knew his friends had suffered because he had died and they were now in danger. But he – and they – knew he had followed through on his convictions and his love of God. And his joy was full, complete. We share that joy when we come through rough times and know we have been faithful to what is good, true and God-given.

Lord, let me know your joy
in my efforts to do what is right;
deepen within me the joy of doing good.

December 11 HOPE IN THE WORK FOR JUSTICE

Br Roger of Taizé writes: 'Bearers of fragility and of radiance, human beings are never irrevocably doomed to the darkness of despair. Even in a life overwhelmed by trials, hope can be perceived.' Among people who suffer injustice, hope is the grace looked for. Refugees look for hope in a way home and the help of other nations; people who have been robbed or abused look for touches of hope and confidence; parents fighting to maintain family values and contact with their children need hope in community and in the church. Jesus found hope in the scriptures, in prayer, and in the community of disciples he led and formed. He shared his hope in the Eucharist and in healing. We can find hope in the same ways.

Lord, may we find hope always in trials;
in the care of others
and in you closeness to us.

December 12 WITNESS TO FAITH

We all go through times when faith is weak. Or we are part of a culture or a people where faith is weak. It effects our belief in God and our belief in ourselves. Where faith in God is weak, faith in each other also is weak. In such times we need witnesses of faith: people whose lives of faith give some life to us. Mary is one such person. A big figure of Advent. One of her principal titles would be 'woman of faith'. Her whole vocation in life was based on a mystery of faith: that she was the mother of God, and that Jesus, who would grow up in her house and in the care of Joseph, was the son of God. All who were associated with her were touched by the light of that faith and lived in the protection of its shadow. It was a faith born in doubt and trouble, as well as in moments of deep certainty, and she knew the struggles of faith that all of us have. Was it any easier for her to believe in God-the-baby than it is for us to believe in God-the-Man?

Lord Jesus, may each time I think of your mother
be for me a moment of faith,
now and at the hour of death.

December 13 WITNESS IN THE CHURCH

We witness to the gospel of Jesus in our individual life, and also in our church life. Our church as a community and an institution is to show its Christian marks: in its compassion for the individual, its prayer to God and its work for justice. We witness as a community of disciples and as individuals. Our church is the community which highlights, for example, the rights of the refugee and the call for compassion to those who may not fall within the social welfare system. Our church points to values beyond money, reputation and power, in the personal lives of individuals and in the public life of its institutions. And this is always within the context of weakness and of sin: weakness and sin in its own members and in the world.

Lord may we your people
act justly, love tenderly
and walk humbly with you.

December 14 GOD WANTS RECONCILIATION

The wish for peace in the world or in a family is an 'expensive' wish, because it means some sort of 'letting go'. If peace is to be found, both parties have to let go of something. Hurts and let-downs in a family, long bitterness in a people. To live in peace in marriage compromises must be made, and compromises in the name of love are better called sacrifices. The ultimate sacrifice of Jesus was the sacrifice of his very life – to create a space of reconciliation between God and ourselves. That space is our very humanity. In each of us is a desire for peace – and then a willingness for reconciliation. Jesus sums up that desire for reconciliation within himself. Reconciliation in a family, a friendship, a nation, is the will of God.

Lord, your kingdom come,
the kingdom of peace and reconciliation;
your will be done.

December 15 GOD'S CARE

They sit around with a list of names every week. They pray before they go out, wonder how much they have and what they can give. They are the men and women of the Society of St Vincent de Paul, who care enough for society to see that hungry people have food and children have toys at Christmas. They are meeting weekly in parishes, schools and other places throughout the world. They try to make Christmas last. In their work, Jesus calls. Among our motives for helping others is that Jesus suffers in his people, and that he would try to help them himself. That God is father and mother and cares actively for us all. To hear Jesus' call in the poor – this is their motivation. Jesus now has no other hands but ours to do his work, no other coins and notes but yours. Your cheque book is his, your credit card, your bit of extra cash – the only means he has for his people today.

Lord, you cry out in the needs of people;
let me hear your cry in their cry,
and feel your sympathy for them.

December 16 MANGER CHILDREN

We visited a school in the Calcutta slums, beside the city rubbish dump. An image of Bethlehem came to mind and will always be part of Christmas: the school – three simples wattle rooms, full of children, all poor, all looking to learn, in a classroom manger. The teachers – shepherds – were from many countries, shepherds transformed within by some vision of a better world, a conviction about education and the value of each child. They were transformed into wise men and women, who had journeyed by an everyday star. Some shepherds came from another land, teachers, and return now, Magi-like, to their own home by another route. The star of the Magi nightly can lead us to mangers and shepherds in the most unexpected of places.

Lord, the value of each child
is reflected in your face;
and each is a sign of the hope of God.

December 17 CHRISTMAS ALL YEAR

Something happens at Christmas that can deepen our lives. Like for the shepherds – the ordinary night was glorified, and they were changed. Christmas means we get in touch with the glory of being a human being, because the glory of God is seen and touched among us. It's good to give that a chance to sink in. We can forget it – criticising people, looking at their faults, using them for our own purposes, denying them their rights. At Christmas the child who is God fills the empty crib with dignity, paints the empty sky with stars, fills the lonely heart with love, and all is the gift of God. Christmas, because of a child, raises us all up, and does the heart good. Christmas, because of each other, raises us all up, and does the heart good. Christmas, because of God, raises us all up, and does the heart good.

Lord, you brighten our lives
you enhance our dignity,
for your are the light of the world.

December 18 SMILE IN POVERTY

The hovel was small and clean, and you'd have to stoop to get into it. Food was scarce in the monsoon rains and the place was damp. But there were smiles. In the middle of the hardship men, women and children found reason to look at each other and the smile was the smile of love. A smile which money cannot buy, nor poverty destroy. This is the love of Bethlehem which parents know and children know. It's the presence of God gently invading even the worst of places. There would probably be more happiness if there were both love and prosperity, but the prosperity of the world can distract from what is truly valuable. It's the joy of the child at Christmas when the present – tiny, simple and cheap – is what was really wanted and the expensive gift is ignored. Love is stronger than death, than poverty, than destitution.

Lord, your Bethlehem home is a home of love,
known and felt in the scarcity of human resources,
but in the plenty of what really matters.

December 19 SOMEONE TOLD ME

A preacher used tell a gospel story, and having told the story well would say, 'I wasn't there myself but someone who was there told me.' That's the way for us. We were not at Bethlehem, nor at Cana nor Tabor nor Calvary. But someone who was there brings us into the mystery and we can ourselves be involved in the midst of the events of Jesus' life. The gospel is history, and mystery. Witnesses of the gospel invite us into the mystery of Jesus' death and resurrection, which is still a reality today. Where people give birth, God gives life; where people join in a wedding celebration, God is present. Where people grow in holiness like the apostles on Tabor, God is present. We are witnesses to each other of the mystery of Jesus' life, and so we can say, 'I wasn't there myself but somebody told me.' God is present in each of us: we tell each other this truth in word and in deed.

Lord Jesus, shine through my life;
speak through my words,
console through my care.

December 20 A MARKER EVENT

Some events change the course of history, and we celebrate this change. The first Christmas is one of these 'marker-events', marking something new happening or coming into the world. God and humanity have a new closeness because of the Incarnation. Men and women are brothers and sisters in a new way because of the Incarnation, and we look on the poor in a new compassionate way because of the poor Christ, the shepherds and the poverty of anyone 'who found no room in the inn'. The change of outlook of Christmas is a change for every day, and in whatever way we make the coming of Christ alive today, we are part of the event that changed human history totally, and changes human history partially every day.

Lord, make us glad to know of the Incarnation,
desirous of making this Incarnation present today,
and committed to serving as you served.

December 21 PEACE

People of every generation have been touched by the story that on the feast of Jesus' birth, men in the trenches of war came out and sang hymns, greeted each other and sometimes exchanged small gifts. Somehow in the middle of killing, terrible living conditions and battles for victory, Christmas highlighted our universal wish for peace; and peace was enjoyed, even for a moment. Some say that the ordinary soldiers in a war desire peace more than the generals. Whatever the reality of battle, the message of Christmas peace is strong. The greatest desire of the ordinary man and woman is for peace to allow family to develop, love to grow, justice to be created, and that we can get on with the ordinary business of life. That is our millennium prayer – peace among God's people in all parts of the world.

Lord, make us people of peace,
in the ordinary relationships of life,
and give peace to all who are at war.

December 22 TALK AN EVERLASTING WORD

Some words we hear remain with us, like an echo in the heart. We remember the tones of one we love as important things were said. Or, for example, we say to someone, 'I always remember what you said the day my child was sick and in danger.' Words can heal, can console, can last forever, like the song says, 'Talk an everlasting word, and dedicate it all to me.' That's the word of God, a word that lasts forever, and dedicated to the whole world and each person in the world. The word of God is a message and even more it is a person. We celebrate the birth of a word that is forever spoken, eternally sung, always new in every century, culture and heart. A word that keeps the soul young and alive. And like the loving words of friendship or marriage, the word of God takes its home in the hearts of each of us.

Lord, your word is truth and life,
your word is joy and comfort
and calls us into service and gratitude.

December 23 LEVEL GROUND

An image often used about life is that it is not a level playing field. Some, born in poverty or other need, begin life walking uphill, or stumbling uphill. Others are born into a loving family, or into wealth, or sufficient security to give a good start. Jesus' path was uphill; he was born into a family of faith, but he was born in poverty, thus choosing to identify with the poor. He was born away from home, and very soon had to flee for his life from his home country, identifying with the refugee. From this upbringing of love and of struggle, and from his life 'hidden with the Father' he grew in wisdom, in compassion and in conviction about his life's mission. Many today face an uphill struggle from even before the moment of birth. The church recommits itself each year and each century to being the voice of the poor, and the defender of the oppressed.

Lord Jesus, may we in our lives
act justly, love tenderly
and walk humbly in your footsteps.

18

December 24 AND WHO IS JOSEPH?

Maybe Joseph is the forgotten person in the birth of Jesus. He may be seen as a quiet, rather confused and elderly companion to Mary. Yet this was a man who loved Mary, and wanted to marry her. He looked forward in his own way to the birth of Jesus. He shared Mary's anticipation, as any father awaiting the birth of a child. His faith had been tested and had grown over the nine months of Mary's pregnancy. Maybe his love was tested, for love is often tested as a man waits for his wife to give birth. She is involved not only with him now, but with her unborn baby. Both love each other in their love for their child. Joseph's love for Mary was seen also in his love for her child soon to be born. Many of us are like Joseph – men and women who are present, sometimes silently, sometimes actively, as Jesus Christ is born again today.

Lord Jesus, child of God, son of Mary,
yesterday, today and forever,
have mercy on us, as we wait for your birth.

December 25 A BIG BIRTHDAY

Did Mary or Joseph ever think we'd be celebrating the birthday of their child twenty centuries later? They were lovingly involved in the mystery of their child, and confident in his future. All of our children are promises for the future – promises that life goes on, and that we last beyond our mortal life. Christianity itself always promises a future – a future of hope, of fulfilment and of God. We need this promise and Christmas each year links us with the past and the future: we know that as Christ was born in Bethlehem, he will be born each year among us, and indeed each day. Our millennium celebration of Jesus' birth invites a promise from each of us that our following of Jesus will last beyond the first day of a millennium, and our commitment is to share his love and gospel each day. Christmas is for a day, Christianity is for every day.

Lord, welcome among us;
and in welcoming you,
we welcome everyone as a child of God.

December 26 AFTER THE BIRTH

After a big celebration comes some peace and quiet. And after the big expectation of the birth of Jesus came the acceptance for Mary and Joseph of the child Jesus. Bethlehem is presented as an excited place: the song of the angels and the visit of the shepherds. There were also the quiet times when Mary looked on Jesus; like any mother, examined him, loved him. Christian life has its times of quiet – contemplative enjoyment of the presence of God. As Mary pondered in her heart what the shepherds had said, she enjoyed her child. As she spent time in quiet contemplation of Jesus, she knew that God was present with her and within her. She was in touch with the glory of God as she gazed on Jesus. And when we are present in love for and with each other, we are in touch with the glory of God.

Lord be glorified in us;
let us know that in the heart of your people
you are present in glory.

December 27 EUCHARISTIC JUSTICE

In Zambia education is no longer free. The money paid back by Zambia in repayments for debt has meant that education and healthcare budgets have been cut. Life expectancy has fallen in 6 years from 54 to 42, and even with the incidence of AIDS, this is a big fall. Discipleship of Jesus includes a concern about the abolition of debt for the third world, for the bread of life, offered by Jesus, is the bread of justice. We are eucharistic people, because we have been given the Eucharist, and are called in the Eucharist to create with Jesus a world of justice. The Eucharist is not a reward of moral and Christian behaviour, not just the gift of food for the journey – it is also a call to justice. When we see some of the poverty of other countries, we would really want to cancel their debt to the wealthy world to benefit the poor.

Lord Jesus, may your bread
give nourishment for the journey of life,
and may it be shared with all in care and justice.

December 28 CIRCLE OF LOVE

When we are giving of ourselves in love and friendship, or in service of the poor, we are in the circle of God's love. We need God's support for love. We know that it can touch into both selfishness and selflessness. Our jealousies, envies, personal needs, effect the way we love. The goodness of another can bring out the best in us. A realisation that God is part of all love also brings out the best in us. We know it can be frightening to love another person very deeply. We can lose ourselves in loving another, or lose the other person through drifting apart or through death. It helps to know that each of us has a bit of God in us, that God wants to nourish the best desires we have to love. That when we get stuck or misunderstand each other, even if we break up or move on, God looks after us, and what we find of God with another person is never lost.

Lord Jesus, be the third in every love,
the source of every friendship,
our hope in times of stress.

December 29 FULFILLED PROMISE

Many expected the coming of Jesus with great hope. Maybe they thought that he would bring freedom, or improve their lives. Maybe they didn't know what exactly would happen. They were overjoyed to see the child and like Simeon and Anna, to take him in their arms. We can wonder did people talk later to Jesus about knowing him as a child and teenager, or being part of his family. Jesus saw farther than these very close and important family relationships. Happiness and discipleship is in hearing the word and recognising him. He said later that many prophets wanted to see what his disciples saw, and later that those who believe and do not see are the happiest. We are the ones now of the fulfilment – people of the promise, for we see and hear what many wanted to see and hear: the Word of God made flesh.

Lord, teach us
to recognise you in the hopes and despairs of your people,
to hear you in the joys and sorrows of your people.

December 30 SON OF GOD, SON OF MARY

Mary is the one who brought the Light to the world. The Irish call Jesus the Son of Mary *(Mac Mhuire)*, and call Mary the mother of God *(Máthair Dé)*. Humanity and divinity, the life of heaven and the life of earth, are mingled in the body of Mary and the child Jesus. The human and divine are mingled in a mother's care, as they are in the care of the millions of mothers and fathers who have spread the light of faith, love and hope in their families and neighbourhoods. They have shone the light of Jesus Christ beyond their family too – voluntary carers of the elderly, and the ones who, by their work for young people over the years, have handed on a better life to the next generation.

Mary, mother of God, bring us to Jesus;
Jesus, son of Mary, bring us to God.
Jesus, Mary and Joseph, care for us
now and at the hour of death.

December 31 ENDINGS

As we extinguish a candle at the last sunset of the second millennium, we are aware that all endings – whether personal like at the end of the forties or fifties, or worldwide like the millennium – are never final for the Christian. As the sun sets on this day for the last time on the millennium, we are reminded of our fragility and our mortality. And in any reminder of mortality and weakness, we are reminded of the light of the world that is neither fragile nor temporary, though strong and gentle. For God and love last forever. The love of the last millennium will light the candle for the next millennium. This love of God in Jesus, the Light of the World, will be the foundation of the new world of peace and justice.

Lord, light that shines in the darkness,
let this light shine in our hearts,
and will know that you are God among us.

January 1 A NEW YEAR

Jesus was always aware that the future was bright. He looked through death to resurrection, through pain to healing, and to the good in everyone, no matter how they seemed to themselves or to others. Christians are people with a future: no failure in life is final, no hurt unmanageable, no bad time without its seeds of growth. A new millennium is nothing magical: will our lives be all that much different today than yesterday? No, and Yes! It is a day for saying our creed of the future: that we believe always in goodness, justice, love and God. We believe that if there are enough good desires for the betterment of the world, something good will always happen, at our time or at God's time. Jesus was fully aware of the pain, injustices and struggles of good people, and always aware also that after three days he would rise again.

Lord Jesus, may I live this year with you;
may you live this year in me,
with your promise of love that is eternal.

January 2 HOPE

We get hope from people who have shared similar experiences as ourselves. When we share our experiences and how we got through them, we are sharing hope. If love breaks up, we may ask someone, 'Did that ever happen to you?' Or the same at a time of death or sickness. We go to people who got through things to find hope for ourselves. Hope comes to us in the ordinary friendships and relationships of life, from those who love us and care for us, and may be communicated with a word, a letter, joke, a smile, a prayer for another or prayer together, Mass or sacraments. We can all be carriers of hope. Hope is seen in small gestures of care and interest in each other, especially at bad times. We look ahead and know we always have a future, the future of Jesus Christ, born among us.

Lord, thanks for those who give hope
in the way they give encouragement
especially in times of great need.

January 3 ORDINARY AGAIN

There were high times in the life of Jesus when the people with him said things like 'it is good for us to be here.' Celebration times like the wedding at Cana, or big spiritual moments like the glory of Tabor, or tough moments when he said he would be killed and raised from death – moments to remember. But most of their time with Jesus was ordinary. Learning from him, enjoying friendship, hearing the call to follow him, being present with him with the sick and the needy. His call would make them happy some days, fearful other days. Our following of Jesus is mostly ordinary. 'Millennium days' are few. Life returns to the ordinary after any big occasion. In the ordinary loves and joys, struggles and boredom, excitements and fears of our lives, we find Jesus as friend and teacher. The ordinary becomes extraordinary.

In all that is ordinary, Lord,
let me see your hand and hear your word,
and discover your will for my life.

January 4 REASON FOR LIVING

A big word for Jesus was 'life'. His reason for coming among us is put: 'I have come that you may have life and have it to the full.' He lived in the heart of God and knew the joy and the exhilaration of life shared with the Father and the Spirit. We don't understand much of the inner life of Jesus, as the life of God is enfolded in mystery. But we know something of the life of God in times of deep love, reconciliation, courage and trust. The life Jesus shares with us is the life of the soul, and this gives strength to the body and joy to the heart. We find a reason for living in our grateful openness to the gift of life in Jesus and in finding deeper meaning through all our life in the relationships we have with him, as he found life to the full in his relationship with God his Father.

Jesus, thank you for life.
Father, share with us your life.
Spirit, share the life of God today.

January 5 LIGHT AMONG LIGHTS

There are many lights offering guidance. The care of people, as in the church and other groups in society, is a principal light. The light of care cannot go out. John, the one who announced the coming of the light of the world, had seen such lights and knew God was near. Care that gets outside our own little circle to the wider and poorer world is also a light of God. There are forces against the light of Christ – greed, violence, murder. John and those who announced the gospel knew that other forces try to put out the light of God, but the light shines because there are the bits of light in all of us. We share it bit by bit, in our openness in prayer and in our Christian activity, and in our work to build the church of the new millennium.

Lord, be the light that guides us,
the light that guides society,
the light that is stronger than any darkness.

January 6 A WISE JOURNEY

They were wise to search for their Saviour. We have many journeys in life: to physical and emotional maturity, to commitments, to parenthood, and the journey towards God. Our Magi, maybe three or more in number, took the journey of faith seriously. And they were not alone: the star they followed was the light of God leading them to God. In fact they had found their God without knowing it, for to search for God is to find God, to want to love God is to love God. We are wise too in how we depict them: from a far country, one of them black, and gift-bearers. For all of us are on the God-journey, rich and poor, of all colours, and nobody is a stranger on that pilgrimage. And all bring gifts: the gift of ourselves, the most precious gift we can give to God.

Take Lord whatever I can offer in your service;
may you be near to us
today and every day.